GROWING MY DIVINE SHRINE

CHERIE NETTLES

ISBN: 978-0-9817608-7-2

Published by

LIFEBRIDGE

BOOKS
P.O. BOX 49428
CHARLOTTE, NC 28277

Printed in the United States of America

DEDICATION

$\mathcal{T}$o Mike, the love of my life, who has taken this journey with me and reminded me to live, love and laugh—even when things were not funny! Thanks for always being by my side—even when this ole' gray mare ain't what she use to be! I love you!

To Alex, my beloved son, you truly are the love of my life and my inspiration—and most of all my "Alexander the Great!" Keep your eyes on Jesus and remember to always live, love, and laugh!

To Ashleigh, my beloved princess and daughter, you will always be beautiful in my eyes! You are my rainbow skies! My princess, keep your eyes on Jesus and remember to always live, love, and laugh!

To Cindy, my beloved best friend, who has truly taken every one of these steps with me—oh, where would I be without you? Let's press on girlfriend—because there really "Ain't no stoppin' us now!"

To Deedle and the Girls! I love you dearly. Girls, always remember to live, love, and laugh!

Finally, and most importantly, to my Savior and lover of my soul, Jesus Christ. Happy Birthday and

3

Merry Christmas—about a decade late—but I praise You that Your mercies are new every day! I truly would be lost without You! Thank You for Your Abundant life—living, loving, and laughing!

I love you all bunches!

— Because He lives, Cherie

Contents

TAKE THE PLEDGE!

*W*hat wonderful childhood memories I have stored away of when I was a Girl Scout. Remember those days, girls? We enjoyed campouts, we sang around the campfire, and proudly recited our pledge. We diligently completed our projects to earn our badges, and made new friends along the way.

My fondest recollection of Scouts was when I first joined. At the entry level I was a Brownie—my favorite time. Well, God does bring us full circle in life because today, well into my forties, my favorite thing to do is eat brownies! Especially the chewy, gooey ones with chocolate icing and a dollop of vanilla ice cream on top. Oh yes, and the hot fudge syrup!

"THE TEMPLE"

It's obvious to me that I have come full circle—especially when I look at my full size pants!

Life takes many crazy turns, but the Lord knows

exactly where He is taking us. As the psalmist wrote, "Your eyes saw my unformed body. All the days ordained for me were written in your book before one of them came to be" (Psalm 139:16).

Then I read in 1 Corinthians 3:16 that our bodies are the temple of God. Since that's the case, then I am not a middle-aged gal putting on a few pounds, battling the bulge—medically known as menopause. Absolutely not. I'm just growing my Divine Shrine!

TIME FOR A NEW PLEDGE

Do you remember holding your right hand in the air with your three fingers pointed up while your pinkie and thumb were closed down?

If you happen to be a male reading this book, please excuse me while I talk to the ladies. I believe we need a new pledge—a Girlfriend's Pledge. We've outgrown our former pledge (I have, in more ways than one. Actually I've outgrown it by about five sizes!). So, I thought I'd write us an updated version.

Do you remember holding your right hand in the air with your three fingers pointed up while your pinkie and thumb were closed down? As young girls we recited: On my honor I

8

promise to do my best. To serve God and my country...

So, using that as our model, let's go!

GIRLFRIEND'S PLEDGE

*On my honor I promise to do my best and
more*
*To eat chocolate, candy, cake and all the things
I adore*
*I promise to stand sister-to-sister, friend-to-
friend and thigh-to-thigh —*
And promise I'll always try
*To stay away from those sizes four, six, eight
and especially a two*
Because to my girlfriends I must always be true!
On my honor I promise to be faithful to you
And do the things that I must do
*That is to stay away from spandex, leotards and
skin-tight jeans regardless the style*
*Because only a girlfriend will walk with you
down every curve and mile!*
So on our honor we will do our best
To grow the temple of God in you and me
And trust in our Holy Trinity

*Because we're not middle-aged gals putting on
    a pound or two
Why, we're putting on more than a few!
We're just embellishing that temple in you and
    me
For our world to see
That we know we're lookin' fine
So on my honor I promise to keep on growin'
    my divine shrine!*

Way to go. We did it! And now we're ready to grow our divine shrines as we fight the good fight— including the battle of the bulge.

Guess what girls. We're gonna win this one!

One

YOU'VE GOT TO BE KIDDING!

*D*on't panic! This isn't a college exam, but I'd like to start with a quiz. Here's a quote from the Bible and I want you to tell me who said it: "God has brought me laughter, and everyone who hears about this will laugh with me" (Genesis 21:6).

When I recently asked an audience if they knew the answer, I had many responses. One person quickly hollered out, "Moses,"—to which I laughed and replied "No way! He was busy building the ark!" My comment confused them even more.

Someone else piped up, "God said it!"

Well, that was a pretty good guess because God did inspire those words. But the correct answer is "Sarah," Abraham's wife.

The story is probably coming back to you, but if not, let me refresh your memory.

Abraham was standing outside his tent chatting with God one day, when the Almighty gave him the big news that he was going to be a father and have a child. He must have thought, "Is God really talking to me? Has He forgotten how old I am?"

But after a few seconds, Abraham knew the Lord *was* speaking directly to him. Now, imagine with me—I call this divine speculation—which means I made it up. But I did get the idea from the Bible.

Remember, in Genesis 15 God promised Abraham he would be the father of many. However, by the time this man was one hundred years old he must have doubted whether God would ever follow through on His promise. What was even harder to believe was that Sarah, his wife, was ninety years old and certainly couldn't bear "many."

There's no fertility drug known to man that could accomplish such a feat, but God said it, God meant it—and we know He *did* it!

BREAKING THE NEWS

Now picture this scene: God tells Abraham he is

going to have as many descendants as the stars in the sky. While Abraham believed God, I just can't help but wonder if he might have asked the Almighty to break that news to Sarah!

If there was a coin toss, Abraham lost. So he went home and told Sarah she was going to have a child. The news could have been worse. Scripture doesn't record that she burst out crying or even threw a frying pan at him—maybe a clay pot or two, but nothing hard enough to really hurt him.

A PREGNANCY TEST?

What was her reaction? She just started laughing! Pretty good ice-breaker, but remember, she had been barren during her childbearing years. Don't you know she wondered why God wanted her to have a baby at ninety? That's why she smiled and said, "God has brought me laughter, and everyone who hears about this will laugh with me" (Genesis 21:6).

— ✃ —

Sarah woke up one morning and felt a wave of nausea wash over her.

Then sure enough, Sarah woke up one morning and felt a wave of nausea wash over her. The next day she felt it again and thought, "Wow, that matzo bread I ate last night must have been past its sell date." But when a similar wave of nausea continued into the third day, she realized she needed to head to the local Wal-Mart pharmacy to pick up a pregnancy test. (Again, this is my loose translation of Genesis 21).

Then she probably returned home to take the early morning test. While impatiently waiting the required five minutes, she yelled out, "Abraham, Abraham, bring me your reading glasses so I can see if there is a pink line on this thing or not. And while you're at it, bring me my teeth. If this thing turns pink— I'm gonna bite you!"

I think the teeth marks were still visible when Abraham was buried!

A SON NAMED "LAUGHTER"

My lay translation is probably not exactly how things happened—but I do know one thing for certain: God did bless Abraham and Sarah with the gift of a son, who they named Isaac (which means "laughter").

Now, some two thousand years later, people still marvel at the hand of God and everyone who hears this biblical account smiles in amazement and awe.

Pregnant at ninety! Now that's a cosmic joke! But God always does the extraordinary through ordinary and obedient people, and He often gives us a laugh or two along the way. Proverbs 17:22 tells us, *"A cheerful heart is good medicine, but a crushed spirit dries up the bones."*

THINK OF THE PERKS!

I'm certain not one guest at Sarah's baby shower had dry bones (or wasn't laughing) because they were probably in stitches as Sarah unwrapped her gifts. Her friends must have been so confused, not knowing whether the diapers were for baby Isaac or Sarah and Abraham!

— ⳥ —

Actually, ninety wouldn't be a bad age to have a child. Just think of the perks.

Actually, ninety wouldn't be a bad age to have a child. Just think of the perks. You'd always be able to sleep through the night. You just wouldn't hear the baby crying because your hearing would be gone!

Also, Sarah would never tire her arms out while nursing. At ninety everything has fallen south. She could have laid Isaac on the floor, sat in the rocker, and nursed him from there! Remember, there is a silver lining in every cloud!

Believe it or not, God has given me plenty to laugh about, and so far people have laughed with me—or at least *at* me. No, I'm not ninety and pregnant, but the Lord has taken the barren circumstances of my life and brought me much joy and happiness.

— ❧ —
*Remember,
there's
a silver
lining in
every cloud!*

A ROLLER COASTER RIDE

In the next couple of chapters I want you to travel with me through a very scary time—my diagnosis of ovarian cancer. In one clean sweep my body was forced into surgical menopause at the age of forty.

Like Abraham probably did, my husband, Mike, has heard me holler a few times since my ordeal—not to bring me his reading glasses, but maybe he has feared I might bite him. However, I think he's learned my bark is usually much worse than my bite. I don't think I've ever really bitten him, but I've threatened to a few times!

Poor dear, he also has to wear a parka under the blankets in bed during the winter because I sleep with the air-conditioning on to combat the night sweats.

He's learned to fasten his "seat-belt of life" securely, in order to hang onto my multiple-personality mood swings—it's a pretty fast roller coaster ride.

All the while he's singing:

"Oh where, oh where did my wife's estrogen go? Oh where, oh where did it go? With her moods that swing and the sweat on her brow, I think she's gonna kill me right now! Oh where, oh where did her estrogen go? Oh where, oh where did it go?"

Bless my husband's heart. As I'm battling the menopausal bulge, I quiz him quite often, "Do I look fat in this?"

He always pleads the Fifth! As a matter of fact, he tactfully avoids this topic as much as possible. I've put on twenty-five pounds since my surgical menopause —now isn't that RICH!

TIME OUT!

Have any of you been there? Or perhaps are there right now? Then travel with me, my friends, through my journey with cancer that has also put me into the battle of the bulge. You may also be calling it menopause, but whatever label you give it, we must replace those terms. Why? Because now we know we're *growing our divine shrines*—not gaining weight. We're just more spiritual than those petite girls!

What I learned during the darkest days of my life has let me know that no matter what valley God allows us to walk through, everything has a purpose. This is why, as you will see in the latter part of this book, I can look at life with a grin instead of a groan, with humor instead of horror, with delight instead of despair.

Before we continue, let's take a little spiritual time out—I'm going to find myself a brownie. What are you craving? Put the book down. I'll be with you in a minute, and then we'll continue on this adventure together—the one that led me to laughter.

I pray you will find many things to smile about along the way.

Two

THE DOCTOR'S IN —I'M OUT!

*O*ctober 19, 2002, started out like every Friday morning—*busy!*

I had to rush the kids off to school—but first had to get them up, dressed, check their book bags, gym bags, pack lunches, and hurry them into the car to start carpool. I had three others to pick up on the way.

Mom's accomplish more by 7:30 A.M. than most people do in a day!

During all this time, my husband—well, was reading the paper. Isn't that rich! Mike's an avid reader. In fact, he is always trying to get me to read! It's not my thing; I don't like to read, never have, and never will. I guess me writing a book is another one of God's cosmic jokes! But let's look on the bright side—I'm not really planning on a series of books. But then again, I have been known to change my mind.

Last Christmas my husband got on a roll and decided that since I was traveling and speaking more than ever, I needed to increase my reading—I guess he wanted me to sound intelligent. I told him that would take a miracle—not a book! Anyway, he wanted to encourage me, so he tucked a ten-dollar Barnes and Noble gift card in my stocking.

I even had enough left over to buy myself a slice of that Snickers Doodle cheesecake.

I went to the bookstore and bought myself a latte! I like this reading thing! I even had enough left over to buy myself a slice of that Snickers Doodle cheesecake. Next year I'm asking Santa for a fifty-dollar card. I may even join a book of the month club. Just think—a new reading card a month. Delicious!

"I LOVED THE MOVIE"

One thing that really gets my goat about readers is that no matter how many times you go to the movies with them, you walk out of the best film you've ever seen, and you are all excited and raving about the movie. Then you look over at your movie companion (that would be my husband or Cindy, my best friend) and exclaim, "I loved the movie! What about you?"

They respond, "Well it was okay, but it wasn't as good as the book."

What? Now you find me a book as exciting as seeing Johnny Depp on a full size movie screen, and I'll personally read it to you!

SOMETHING "UNUSUAL"

Let's be honest, when do I have time for reading? After carpooling, I came home, cleaned the breakfast dishes, packed for a weekend conference where I was to speak, then rushed to the grocery store to make certain my family had everything they needed while I was gone. I would only be away 24 hours, but it looked as if I were stocking a bomb shelter for a year!

I drove home, unloaded the mountain of groceries, gathered all my materials, put the finishing touches on my message, and headed out the door shortly after noon, driving to the women's conference where I was to speak. I planned to be in Spartanburg, South

Carolina, at 2:00 P.M. sharp. The drive would take a little under two hours, so I was sure I would be on time.

My schedule was tight but I knew I could make it as long as I didn't have any major snafu's. Well, there was something else that concerned me.

All morning I had felt an unusual pressure in my right side. It wasn't painful, but out of the ordinary. Ladies, you know what is usual, and what is not.

I thought maybe I might have the onset of a bladder infection.

MY SELF-DIAGNOSIS

Before driving off I looked up my doctor's phone number up and programmed it into my cell phone.

As I got on the road, I noticed the pressure had not subsided. So I picked up my mobile phone and called my doctor's office. He was in—and I was out. Actually I wanted to keep it that way.

I thought I'd give him a sad story of how I was away speaking that weekend, and feared I was coming down with something. And with my self-diagnosed bladder infection, surely he would take pity on me and call in an antibiotic prescription at a drug store in Spartanburg. I could easily drive through a pharmacy pick up window—and that would be that!

My well-thought-out plan was that I could get the medication and be okay by Monday and not have to take the time to go to his office. Plus, he wouldn't have to squeeze in another patient.

"FOLLOW THE DIRECTIONS"

I guess my self-diagnosis wasn't good enough for my doctor! He said, "Cherie, I'll tell you what to take over the counter to get you through the weekend, and then you can come in Monday afternoon when you get back."

Then he added, "If you follow the directions and drink lots of cranberry juice, you'll be fine until then." Some nerve, I thought—why do these male doctors think they can figure out *Who does he think he is? Are physicians smarter than mothers?* more than their female patients. I'd never understand. Who does he think he is? Are physicians smarter than mothers?

To be honest, I'm really thankful doctors don't

listen to us—even when we do have a self-diagnosis-
—and a degree in Secondary Education, I might add!

I went about my whole weekend drinking large swigs of cranberry juice and taking the medicine he recommended, which I loved because it turned my urine bright orange! Now isn't that a nice color for the tidy-bowl man?

I talked on the phone with a girlfriend about hot flashes, but even she knew something wasn't adding up. Of course, I was too young to have one of those!

HE PATIENTLY LISTENED

I made it through the conference no worse for wear and scheduled my appointment for 2:00 P.M. that Monday afternoon. Upon arrival, I tried to explain to my doctor that since I traveled so much with my work, I didn't always have time to come into his office, and that he just needed to listen to me when I phoned in with a symptom.

He laughed! I love my doctor because right there and then he should have put me in a straight jacket and bundled me off to an insane asylum, or at least knocked some sense into me! Instead he just patiently listened as I rambled on about what I was feeling.

THAT LITTLE TOWEL

After our initial conversation, the doctor made a surprising announcement. He had decided he needed to do an examination. He told me to go into Room #1 with the nurse, and he'd be there shortly. When I looked shocked, he said, "Oh, you don't have to take off everything, just everything below the waist." Now, wasn't that nice of him?

"Oh, you don't have to take off everything, just everything below the waist."

I entered the examination room.

Oh, no! I looked at the stirrups— and I'm not even a cowgirl! Before he walked down the hall, he handed me a towel—about the size of a hand towel—and explained that he would be right back as soon as I had covered up. I'm still at a loss to know what he expected me to hide with that tiny towel. The only thing it could have adequately covered up was my pinky toe or maybe my kneecap—but somehow I managed to climb up on the cold plastic table and lay the tiny piece of fabric on top of my private parts.

25

WAS HE KIDDING?

Peeking his head around the door, the doctor asked, "Are you comfortable?"

I knew it! At any moment, Allen Funt was going to pop out and yell, "Surprise! You're on Candid Camera!"

Was I comfortable? Was he kidding? Surely any doctor has more sense than to ask a question like that to a woman lying bottomless on a cold, plastic table, with a hand towel covering a small spot on her body! Was I *comfortable!* Was he kidding?

I kept looking around, but the camera never appeared. So I said, "Not really."

My doctor then added, "This will not take long. Just slide down closer to me so I can do the exam."

If you are a woman reading these words, you know the noise the table makes when you slide barebottomed on a plastic examination table. How embarrassing! I kept apologizing, saying, "That wasn't me! That wasn't me."

He told me, "Just relax. It happens all the time," but did I notice a smirk on his face? Was he laughing at me? Oh sure, just relax, and while I'm doing that, why don't you ask the nurse to get bamboo shoots and drive them into my fingernails. *Just relax?*

HE DIDN'T SEEM CONCERNED

After the exam, he told me to get dressed and come to his office so we could talk. I wasn't worried at all because he didn't seem concerned.

I even walked into his office and jokingly said, "Here, before you give me the results, why don't you undress—just below the waist. Slip this little towel on and just relax, and then we can talk about me."

He laughed out loud. Wow, am I glad he is a good sport, and a fellow church member. As a Christian man, I didn't think he would throw me out of his office!

"IS THIS LIFE-THREATENING?"

Immediately, the doctor became serious and told me, "I'm sorry, but I found a large uterine fibroma, but I'm sure it's benign."

"Fibroma? What's that?" I wanted to know.

He explained that it was a uterine tumor.

"Why are you sorry?" I asked, suspiciously. "Is this life-threatening?"

I didn't hear much of his answer because the only word that grabbed my attention in the previous sentence was *tumor.* From that moment on my mind went completely blank.

He tried to assure me again the tumor was benign, but he was sorry that I would have to undergo a surgical procedure so close to the holidays and be recovering during Christmas.

His plan was to make a midline cut in my abdomen and remove the tumor. "We'll schedule the surgery as soon as possible."

Surgery! I went numb.

THINKING OF THE HOLIDAYS

My doctor understood it would make decorating my home and preparing for the holidays quite difficult. He knew Christmas was a big event at our house because he had delivered and taken care of both our son and daughter, who were eleven and eight years old at the time.

He scheduled the surgery and I headed out of the office.

To shift gears and divert my thoughts, I tried to focus on making a mental Christmas list in my head.

Just as I was leaving, the doctor called out, "Cherie, wait a minute. The sonogram technician is in the office today. Let's have her look at the tumor to determine its size. I usually just go ahead and do the surgery, but this will give us some more information."

I mentally put my list on hold and replied, "Sure."

SHE PUSHED THE "CALL" BUTTON

I headed down the hallway to wait on the technician. My turn finally came up—not as though I really wanted a turn—but I went in for my sonogram.

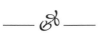

A very concerned look came over her.

She began the procedure and as soon as the image popped up on the screen, I saw the demeanor on her face change. A very concerned look came over her.

She pushed the "call" button and asked my doctor to come into the room immediately. When he walked in they began discussing what was and wasn't on the image. Finally, he commented, "It's not her ovaries; it's her uterus, I'm sure it is."

He looked at me and said, "Cherie, I think we need to run some more tests."

"What kind of tests?" I quickly replied. "Will they hurt?"

He explained it was a simple blood test, and since his technician was the best in the area, we should investigate her findings.

All of this information still didn't sink in. After all, I was thinking about Christmas.

He continued by telling me that he really felt the mass on my uterus was benign. Well, since I didn't need my uterus any more, getting rid of the monthly thing might be a good idea!

He wanted to do one more blood test. The test was a CA-125, which meant even less to me at the time.

THE PHLEBOTOMIST

Zoning in on my mental holiday check list, I reminded myself I would need to purchase two red sweaters for our Christmas card picture. Then I heard my name called out.

I went over to the lab, and the phlebotomist (How do you like my medical vocabulary? You know the person that draws blood) was calling my name. She drew a sample, and I headed out of the office for home.

I guess my blood went to the lab from there, but marked ASAP. I've learned since then a CA-125 is a very important ovarian cancer indicator test, especially when a sonogram shows a tumor on a patient's ovary.

On my drive home, I stopped by Bojangles' for chicken strips to serve for dinner to my husband and the kids that night, with a large iced tea for me.

All that poking and prodding had worn me out—at least that was my story for not fixing dinner that night, and I'm sticking to it!

All that poking and prodding had worn me out.

"ARE YOU SURE?"

I really didn't think much more about the test results.

Two days later, on Wednesday night after church the phone rang, My husband told me, "It's the doctor."

"Why is he calling? was my first response. But I knew I had to talk to him.

When I picked up the receiver, he began, "Cherie, how are you doing?"

I responded, "Are you at work or at home? Because if you are at home, I am concerned."

He said, "I'm home and my wife's right here beside me." She was one of my sorority sisters.

Then he added, "I need to talk with you about your blood test. It came back elevated."

"Are you sure?" I answered. And a cold sweat broke over me.

"Yes," he said, "and I need you to see another doctor.

Concerned, I asked, "Elevated? What does that mean?"

He responded, "The number is over 400."

Since that meant absolutely nothing to me, I wanted to know, "What should it be?"

"Below 30."

Whew! This didn't sound good. "What doctor are you sending me to?"

After he gave me the name, I continued, "What kind of doctor is he?"

"Cherie, he is a GYN Oncologist. And he needs to see you Friday morning."

I began to weep, immediately thinking about my two wonderful children and my husband.

I CLOSED MY EYES

The next day, on Thursday, my doctor was going to send me to the hospital to have more tests run. The results would be delivered ASAP to my new doctor, the GYN Oncologist, for my appointment the next morning. I quizzed him, "You want to see if it has metastasized don't you?"

He told me they wanted to make sure I was healthy enough for surgery.

I closed my eyes and prayed, "Lord, tell me what is happening? What will tomorrow hold?"

Three

"Good Morning, Cherie"

*A*s a little girl I loved the nursery rhyme: *Humpty Dumpty sat on a wall. Humpty Dumpty had a great fall. All the king's horses and all the king's men couldn't put Humpty Dumpty together again.*

Now I was a big girl—and was literally falling to pieces. I was crying myself to sleep, and before going in for the additional tests, I was sobbing until my body had the *snubs*—you know, when you shake from head to toe because you've cried so hard.

In my head, I knew the promises of God's Word, but my emotions had taken over and my heart had no understanding that day.

In preparation for a CT scan that Thursday, I had to drink that awful chalky mixture for the doctor to be able to see my insides. I took small sips, and cried between swallows.

About ten minutes after I finished drinking the required chalk, a technician hooked up the IV fluids and asked me to lie flat on the table that would soon slide me into the scanner. I couldn't lie still. My snubs had caused my entire body to continue shaking.

Tears flowed as I clenched my fists. The technician asked me again to lie still, but I couldn't.

Finally, she said, "What's the matter?"

All I could do was open my fists, and when I did two pictures fell out of my hands. They were of my two children. Distraught, I looked at her and exclaimed, "How can God do this to me?"

She quickly realized I wasn't going to calm down, so she had the doctor order Xanax to help me relax. Have you ever taken Xanax? We would have world peace tomorrow if everyone took that pill!

After the scans, I went home with my husband, but continued to plead, "God how can You do this to me?"

IT'S OKAY TO QUESTION

Have you ever asked God that question or

something similar? For example, have you prayed, "Why me?"

It's perfectly okay to ask God why. It's human nature to be scared, it's even okay to be angry with God (He's secure with who He is) and question what He is doing. But it is never okay to stop talking to your heavenly Father.

_____ ❦ _____

Even when all the horsemen can't put us together again—the King can!

As long as you are questioning God, you are communicating with Him.

Even when all the horsemen can't put us together again—the King can!

SURGERY—ON HALLOWEEN?

At lunch that day, I was still weeping. I looked at my husband and asked him a tough question: "Mike, if they cut me wide open and they come in and say there is nothing we can do, is God still good?"

Mike was silent, yet it spoke volumes. He didn't have to answer because he knew who my Rock was and that beneath my tears, my faith had a solid foundation.

Together, we went to the surgeon's office on Friday and my husband explained to him that he was an engineer and a numbers man. He explained that he just wanted an educated percentage of my chances of having cancer (now he's not a betting man—he is a good old Southern Baptist).

The doctor said he was 90% sure it was not cancer, but he could not make any guarantees.

During this time I learned that Dr. Smith was one of the leading oncologists in the nation—and consults with surgeons worldwide in his specialty.

Surgery was scheduled for the following Thursday —Halloween. It was the first time I had not seen my children in their Halloween costumes and it was breaking my heart.

"WE'LL GET THROUGH THIS"

Not wanting to alarm the kids, we were particularly upbeat that morning as we got them off to school. But then I sat down on the couch and the tears erupted. I thought they would never stop.

Mike came and sat beside me to offer comfort, but he was crying too.

He opened the Bible and read from the Psalms. "Find rest, O my soul, in God alone; my hope comes from him. He alone is my rock and my salvation; he is my fortress, I will not be shaken. My salvation and my honor depend on God; he is my mighty rock, my refuge" (Psalm 62:5-7).

He took my hand, looked into my eyes, and calmly assured me, "Cherie, we'll get through this because God truly is our refuge."

"WILL SHE LOSE HER HAIR?

At the medical center, they gave me some Valium and I was—well slowly drifting away.

Next, they put me in a hospital gown and those flimsy little slippers. I was practically buck naked!

Friends from the church were stopping by and in my half-dazed state, I waved them in. But the nurses politely told them, "You'll have to stop by after the surgery."

Three and a half hours later, the surgeon came out to the waiting room.

Three and a half hours later, the surgeon came out to the waiting room and told Mike, "Cherie has ovarian cancer. It's a class 3C. I have just done a complete hysterectomy."

If you know anything about cancer there are 4 stages, with 4 being the most serious.

Dr. Smith continued, "It has metastasized in all of

her pelvic area and has also spread into her stomach, and I removed he top layer, the omentum." Then he added, "She will begin an aggressive form of chemotherapy two weeks from today. If we wait too long, she won't be strong enough."

Mike asked. "Will she lose her hair?"

"With this amount of chemo, I think she probably will."

"NO VISITORS"

When I "came to" in recovery, I knew that no matter what the news was, I could face it because I had already been to my strong source of strength, my Rock.

_____ ✀ _____

I looked at the surgeon and knew, "I have cancer, don't I?"

In my room, my best friend was rubbing my feet, my husband was holding my hand, and my doctor was stroking my face.

I looked at the surgeon and knew, "I have cancer, don't I?"

He replied, "Yes, you do. But it's treatable, and God willing it is curable."

I never had such attention as I received in that

hospital. Man, did they ever wait on me. I didn't have to cook once or even make a bed!

On November 4, I was a little more coherent than I had been and all around me things were calm and peaceful. The nurses were no longer hovering over me, and the "No Visitors" sign was still hanging on my door.

Mike arrived and continued to read the Psalms to me.

A WORD JUST FOR ME

Mike was wonderful. The next morning he was there again, reading more Scriptures. When he left, however, I was desperate for assurance and began begging God for a specific word that was just for me alone. All that seemed to come to mind was, "Be still, and know that I am God" (Psalm 46:10).

But I needed more: "Lord, that's not the word I want."

He quietly told me, "But that's the word you're getting."

That evening, Mike phoned and, rather excited,

_____ &⃯ _____ told me, "I think I've found just what

I quickly you need. Read Psalm 86."

turned the   I quickly turned the pages of my
pages of my Bible and devoured every word. It felt
Bible and like the psalmist had penned these
devoured words just for me:
every word.

Hear, O Lord, and answer me, for I am poor and needy. Guard my life, for I am devoted to you. You are my God; save your servant who trusts in you. Have mercy on me, O Lord, for I call to you all day long. Bring joy to your servant, for to you, O Lord, I lift up my soul.

You are forgiving and good, O Lord, abounding in love to all who call to you. Hear my prayer, O Lord; listen to my cry for mercy. In the day of my trouble I will call to you, for you will answer me.

Among the gods there is none like you, O Lord; no deeds can compare with yours. All the nations you have made will come and worship before you, O Lord; they will bring glory to your name. For you are great and do marvelous deeds; you alone are God.

Teach me your way, O Lord, and I will walk

in your truth; give me an undivided heart, that I may fear your name.

I will praise you, O Lord my God, with all my heart; I will glorify your name forever. For great is your love toward me; you have delivered me from the depths of the grave...Turn to me and have mercy on me; grant your strength to your servant and save the son of your maidservant.

Give me a sign of your goodness, that my enemies may see it and be put to shame, for you, O Lord, have helped me and comforted me (Psalm 86:1-17).

Wow! Reflecting on that marvelous passage, I drifted into a deep, sound sleep at about 11:30 P.M.

A VOICE FROM HEAVEN

At four in the morning, November 6, 2002, I woke up in my hospital room and heard a beautiful, still-quiet voice saying, "Good morning, Cherie. I want you to be confident in Me and be at peace, for there is no more cancer."

I love to personalize Scripture. So I picked up my

journal and began to write Psalm 86 in my own words. I took the phrase, "You have delivered me from the depths of the grave," and wrote, "Daddy, I am climbing up in Your lap. Save me from the grave, because no one else can. Only You."

Then I wrote down what He had spoken, telling me to put my confidence in Him and be at peace, for there is no more cancer.

Then with a renewed faith, I closed my eyes to rest.

"WHAT ARE YOU SAYING?

At 6:00 A.M., Dr. Smith threw open the door, and like a rooster, woke me up and with an exuberant, "Good morning!"

I could hardly believe what he said next: "Cherie, I have good news for you."

"What is it?" I wanted to know.

"It's not what I told you earlier. Your tumor is what we call non-invasive."

That sounded good, but I needed to know more. "Exactly what are you saying?"

With great confidence, he said, "It means it can't spread. And if it can't spread, it can't kill you."

I smiled and asked Dr. Smith, "Would you let me

read my journal to you?"

He is a God-fearing man and replied, "Absolutely."

I told him how at four o'clock in the morning God woke me up with these words: "Good morning, Cherie. I want you to be confident in me and be at peace, for there is no more cancer."

He took me in his arms, gave me a gentle kiss on my cheek and told me, "God has smiled on you."

—— ॐ ——

"God has smiled on you."

"DEAR CHERIE"

Two days later I received a letter from my friend, Linda. She has a health condition that takes more energy for her to get out of bed in the morning than you and I exert in a whole day.

Her letter was dated November 6, 2002.

"Dear Cherie," she began. "I woke up this morning at 3:30 A.M. and God placed you on my heart. I have continued to pray for you all morning and it is now about 4:45 A.M. I have been taking a Bible study called "Let Prayer Change Your Life." And I have been learning to listen to God.

The letter continued, "I have discovered in this

study that when I am hearing from God, He nudges me. And if I am obedient, in most cases He shows me what is going on. I'm not sure what the urgency is this morning, but He told me to write you."

Then she explained how God had impressed upon her to pray for me at that specific time.

THAT'S ALL I NEEDED TO KNOW

It was more than mere coincidence. At the very minute God was telling me there was no more cancer, He awakened my friend Linda to pray on my behalf. It was part of the Father's perfect timing.

When God performs a miracle, He invites His servants to attend. As He tells us, "Call to me and I will answer you and tell you great and unsearchable things you do not know" (Jeremiah 33:3).

I don't have all the answers, but thankfully God does. And when He assured me the cancer was gone—that's all I needed to know.

Four

YOUR DADDY'S HOME—TO STAY

*O*ne day, when I was in the fourth grade, I was visiting my friend Vicki's house. As we were playing, music was drifting from the radio, when she suddenly exclaimed, "Shhhh, this is my favorite song."

As I listened, I became completely mesmerized by the lyrics—and wanted to hear them again and again. I will never forget the words:

You're my love, you're my angel
You're the girl of my dreams.
I'd like to thank you for waiting patiently
Daddy's home, your Daddy's home to stay.
How I've waited for this moment
To be by your side.

Your best friend wrote and told me
You had teardrops in your eyes.
Daddy's home, your Daddy's home to stay.

For years, I remembered and sang the words of that song, just waiting for the moment when my own Daddy would come home—but, sadly, he never did.

I wish I could tell you how I was raised in a wonderful, peaceful, perfect home, but that is far from reality. My alcoholic father abandoned our family when I was just two years old.

From that moment forward, there was a huge gaping hole in my heart—as well as in the hearts of my brothers, sister, and mother. Our lives were soon spinning out of control.

A FAKE SMILE

It seemed that we moved every time the rent was due. My mom had the painful decision to choose between paying the electric bill or providing dinner for her four children who were desperately seeking love, approval, blessing, and provision.

Drugs, alcohol, and promiscuity became common-place in my home. I grieved everyday—hurting and screaming on the inside, but painting a fake smile on my face to fit in with the other little girls.

As time passed, my heart grew hardened and my hope began to diminish. Whenever I heard the words of that song, I had to choke back the lump rising in my throat. Why couldn't I be my father's angel, the little girl of his dreams? Why couldn't I—just one time—feel his strong arms wrap around me?

Why couldn't I be my father's little angel, the girl of his dreams?

Later, things grew worse, much worse. My mother became unemployed, we were evicted from our home, and there was a drug bust at our apartment.

"WHERE IS HE?"

Late one night (way past my bedtime) a knock came at our door. My brother ran and said, "It's them!"

Mom calmly walked to the door, opened it slowly so there was only a small crack. Immediately, the door was violently shoved open.

Tearfully, I stood behind my mother. A woman's voice yelled, "Where is he?"

They were searching for my 13 year-old brother. I looked and saw this intruder holding a knife and a young man behind her was carrying a bat.

"He isn't here," mom replied.

The woman then threatened, "I will kill all of you if you don't bring him to the door."

I crawled under the covers and began to cry.

Reluctantly, my mother agreed only if she could stay with him. They closed the door and I went to my tiny walk-in closet (with a twin bed), crawled under the covers and began to cry.

"I NEED A DADDY"

I'm not certain what took place outside, but I do know this: I cried out, "God if you are my Father—prove it! I need a Daddy. I need to crawl up in your lap. Save us, and please let me go to sleep and wake up to see the morning."

For the first time in my life I pictured God in Heavenly white garments sitting in a huge rocking chair, gently reaching down to pick me up and tenderly place me on His lap. With that comforting image in mind, I drifted off to sleep.

The sun was extraordinarily beautiful the next morning. I was reassured that I did have a Daddy and even if I didn't know it, I had prayed words from Holy Scripture.

It was much later that I learned Jesus Christ, our Lord and Savior also called out to "Abba" Daddy in His time of need. From His cross, Jesus cried, "Abba, Father...everything is possible for you. Take this cup from me. Yet not what I will, but what you will" (Mark 14:36).

That night, I asked God to be with me and I felt His presence—the same God who promised He would never leave us or forsake us (Hebrews 13:5).

A FATHER TO THE FATHERLESS

Scripture teaches us that our heavenly Father is a loving God who desires for us to call Him "Daddy." "For you did not receive a spirit that makes you a slave again to fear, but you receive the Spirit of sonship. And by him we cry, 'Abba, Father' (Romans 8:15).

Today if you are grieving, struggling under the strain of sorrow, you are not alone. Allow God's loving arms to gently and tenderly pick you up and be the Daddy He longs to be. You're never too old to be His child.

Perhaps your father was present in your home but absent in heart. It may be that he was overbearing, unloving, critical, or abusive. Perhaps you are grieving this loss for your own child, relative, or loved one. My precious friend, trust me: God is the Father to the fatherless (Psalm 68:5).

Open the door to your loving Heavenly Father. He will not only enter, but be home to stay.

Five

BEAUTIFUL FEET

I had to chuckle when I read the words of the apostle Paul: "How beautiful are the feet of those who bring good news!" (Romans 10:15).

Beautiful feet? What? Boyfriends and suitors have told me many things in my lifetime, but never that my feet were a thing of beauty. In fact, anyone who said that would be lying! My feet were never pretty, but by the age of 17 there was absolutely no *physical beauty* in them. Don't get me wrong, I'm thankful for my feet; I'm just hoping they're not my best feature!

At 17, I woke up late one December evening to the ring of the telephone. I jumped out of bed and ran through the den, and—bam! Right into the hearth of the fireplace. (Running while groggy is not recommended. And if the furniture has been rearranged for the Christmas tree, you really need to be alert and turn on the light, because smacking your toes on the bricks of a hearth really hurts.)

I hobbled to the telephone, and wouldn't you know it, the caller had hung up. I shuffled back to my bed and took a minute to drift back to sleep because of the throbbing in my toes.

HOPELESS

Little did I know that night would impact the rest of my life; I spent the next two years in and out of doctor's offices, hospitals, and clinics trying to figure out why the inflammation and pain would not subside.

I spent the next two years in and out of doctor's offices, hospitals, and clinics.

Finally, two years and many medications later, I landed in the office of a rheumatologist, a doctor who treats arthritis and other autoimmune diseases.

By this time the pain and inflammation had migrated up my right leg into my knee. It was so swollen I couldn't pull my straight-leg jeans over it, and for a girl of the 1980's, this was a tragedy.

I began to hurt everywhere in my body. My doctors seemed to believe it was some form of arthritis, but were baffled as to what kind. None of my blood work was conclusive. The arthritis appeared to be rheumatoid, but I didn't seem to fit the profile.

After months of treatment, my disease progressively worsened. I withdrew from college and spent most of my 19-year-old days in bed. I felt hopeless.

Was My Life Over?

During one of my routine appointments, the doctor who was treating me at the time explained that my disease had become aggressive, and I needed to prepare for my future. His prognosis was that by age 21, it would cripple me, and I would live the remainder of my years in chronic pain and in a wheelchair.

I left his office sobbing, feeling my life was over. I asked God, "Why?" My dream of college, becoming a teacher, a wife, and a mother seemed to be slipping away. How could God allow this to happen to me? Thinking of marriage and a family, I couldn't become pregnant while taking high-risk medications, and my doctor predicted I would never be able to stop taking these drugs.

After five surgeries and multiple regimens of high-risk, long-term medications later, I thank God I'm still walking! Oh, my toes are deformed, and I walk with a pronounced limp, but I walk!

My feet aren't beautiful by any stretch of the imagination, but they still take me where I want to go.

And about my dreams: in 1984, I graduated cum laude from the University of South Carolina (Go Gamecocks!) with a degree in Secondary education. I became a teacher, and in 1989, married the man of my dreams.

OUR DREAM MAKER

—— ☙ —— In 1990, my disease went into a *I was given* five-year remission, and during that *the okay to* time I came off all of my medications. *try and have* I was given the okay to try to have a *a baby.* baby. And guess what? In February 1991, I gave birth to Alex, the most beautiful baby boy ever (in spite of his cone-shaped head and blue skin.)

Then in 1993, I repeated the process and became the proud mother of the most beautiful baby girl ever—Ashleigh! Wow! God really is a God of miracles.

I prayed for more than 12 years about having a family, and I had no idea of the wonder the Lord was going to bestow on me with my two children. God is our Great Physician, and He can do what man cannot.

Today, you may be suffering from physical or emotional pain. You, too, may feel that your life is over or that your dreams have been snatched from you. Trust me when I say that God is our Dream Maker. Psalm 37:4 teaches us to delight ourselves in the Lord and He will grant us the desires of our hearts.

When faith fades and doubt creeps in think on these words: "Ah, Sovereign Lord, you have made the heavens and the earth by your great power and outstretched arm. Nothing is too hard for you" (Jeremiah 32:17).

Friend, your life is not over. I'm telling you to keep dreaming not because I've read it somewhere, but because *I've walked it!*

Six

I LOVE YOU LIKE THE MOON AT NIGHT

One of my son's favorite bedtime stories was *I Love You, Good Night*, by Jon Buller and Susan Schade. We read it over and over.

The binding and the pages are shredded. We've even worn out the tape that held the binding back together! We'd quote the lines of the book every night before I tucked him in. I would say to Alex, "I love you like pigs love pies."

Then he would reply, "I love you like frogs love flies."

But before I shut the door we would both repeat the last line of the book, "I love you, good night!"

As a matter of fact, occasionally we *still* say some of the lines from this book to one another at bedtime. That really does a mother's heart good!

When my little boy would get scared of the

darkness in his bedroom, I would open the curtains
___ &b ___ and let the moon shine in through his
The "moon" window, and that was one of the
page was reasons the "moon" page was our
one of our favorite. The page read, "I love you
favorites. like the moon at night, big and round
and warm and bright."

NO MORE NIGHT

Have you ever thought just how dark it would be on earth without the glow of the moon at night? Can you imagine a place where no sun or moon is needed?

Well, there is such a place. It's called heaven, where God will be our light.

John describes the beauty of heaven in his vision recorded in Revelation 4. He tells how he saw a throne with One sitting upon it. He described a rainbow, resembling an emerald, that encircled the throne, and there was a sea of glass, clear as crystal.

THE LAMB—THE LAMP

This wondrous place is where I'm living my life to go—to my eternal home with our heavenly Father. It will be beyond comprehension, but one day we, like John, will walk through those gates of pearl and see beauty radiating from the light of God. Yes, "The city does not need the sun or the moon to shine on it, for the glory of God gives it light, and the Lamb is its lamp" (Revelation 21:23).

Until I see these glories face to face, I can look up to heaven and say, "God, I love You like the moon at night, big and round and warm and bright—just like You! I love You Lord. Good night!"

Seven

JUST DROPPING IN

*A*shleigh was in the second grade and her spelling bonus word for week 14 was "miracle."

"M-I-R-A-C-L-E" she carefully spelled it out.

"Good girl," I encouraged her, "try again. Sound it out, "MIR-A-CLE."

"Okay mommy: "M-I-R-A-C-L-E — MIRACLE!"

"You did it!" I exclaimed.

What a big word for such a little girl. We practiced all week and finally the night before her test she had it down pat.

She sat at her small white desk decked in her plaid school girl dress with a red bow holding back her curls, and, when her time came, she correctly spelled the bonus word.

HER SPECIAL SENTENCE

But earlier, when we were practicing, at one point

63

a puzzled look crossed her face. She asked, "Mommy, what is a miracle?"

I quickly responded, "Ashleigh, a miracle is something only God can do. Like heal a sick person, or create a baby in a mommy's tummy, or something else really big and special!"

I saw her little face process the definition, and I just knew a zillion questions would follow, but I was wrong. She moved on to writing her sentences with her spelling words.

After a few minutes she looked up at me and said, "Mommy, do you want to hear my sentence for miracle?"

I smiled. Her face lit up and she read, "Miracle— I am a miracle."

I laughed through tears and told her she was my precious miracle, but wondered if she really understood how God had already performed a miracle in her young life.

A New Family Memeber

When Ashleigh was two years old we went to Myrtle Beach, South Carolina, and decided to take the children (our son, Alex, was five) to the water park.

We had seen advertisements all week lauding the children's play area and knew this would be a great escape from Ashleigh's squeals on the beach—from all of the sand she had eaten or collected in her swim diaper.

It was an especially hot day. The line to enter the water park was long. My husband, Mike, began talking to the family behind us while I was chasing Alex and prying frightened Ashleigh off my leg.

——— ❧ ———

I was chasing Alex and prying frightened Ashleigh off my leg.

The family shared with Mike that they traveled from Ohio every year to vacation in Myrtle Beach. They went on to explain that this year things were different because now they had a new family member. Surprised at the older parents and looking for the baby, the family then told Mike that their great nephew was now the new addition, and that things were a little strained since they had only met him a couple of times.

He was 13 years old and in the past year had lost his mother, had never known his father, and was living with his grandmother, who died unexpectedly. They were the only family members left to care for the boy. So with only two weeks notice this family had a new addition and he was now on his first vacation with them.

OFF TO THE "BIG BOY" SLIDE

Mike smiled at the young man, patted his back, and told him he was in for a fun day. He gave Mike a slight grin.

The woman then told Mike how their great nephew was really not supposed to be on the trip, but because of some unexplained circumstances he was able to join the family much earlier than the courts had anticipated.

We spent much of our afternoon playing on the slides and sitting around "the baby" pools. Alex finally gained a little confidence, so we all headed off to the "big boy" slide which was about five feet tall.

We waved him on as we stood in the water below waiting to catch our brave boy. Ashleigh stood at a careful distance from the slide holding her daddy's leg repeating, "It not my turn! It not my turn!"

We were assured she would not be sliding on this trip!

"WHERE'S ASHLEIGH?"

Alex continued to run in a large circle climbing up, sliding down, and giggling as he landed in the water. It was a blast!

About that time Mike looked at me and asked, "Where's Ashleigh?"

My heart sank! Alex yelled, "Ashleigh, get down!" Mike and I looked up as she climbed the last step of the slide. With complete lack of composure I screamed loudly and Mike ran off to retrieve her; however, trying to run in water you can only go at a slug's pace.

My heart sank! Alex yelled, "Ashleigh, get down!"

When Ashleigh stood up she realized how high on the slide ladder she was and began to scream. Seeing her panic, we all began to call out, "Stand still, Ashleigh. Daddy is coming to get you!"

As soon as Mike reached the edge of the water our worst fears became a reality. In her fright, Ashleigh would not listen and was searching for the fastest way down. She found it! She turned, slipped, and went plummeting head first down the five foot drop heading towards the concrete. I screamed again and fell to my knees. I knew she was going to break her neck.

A PREARRANGED APPOINTMENT

Help was nowhere in sight. Mike hopped out of the pool to the slide, but we all knew he would never make the catch. At that very moment, from absolutely nowhere, arms reached out (chills still run up and down my spine as I think about it) and caught Ashleigh in the nick of time. The young man comfortingly said, "You're okay little girl, here's your Daddy." Mike looked up and to his surprise it was the boy he had met at the entrance gate. Yes, the one who wasn't supposed to be with his new family until September.

"You're okay little girl, here's your Daddy."

The 13-year-old was just standing around the "baby pool" area.

I knew at that moment why the court allowed him to be here early. I knew why he'd come to rest for a minute, and I also knew a tragedy in his life brought him to the water park that day.

DIVINE FOOTSTEPS

There is a wonderful verse in the Old Testament where God declares, "Every place that the sole of your foot shall tread upon, I have given unto you" (Joshua 1:3 KJV).

I firmly believe that God orchestrated the soles of the young man's feet that day so he could be the vessel He would use to perform a miracle and save our daughter's life.

With tears in his eyes, Mike began to profusely thank the young man, and told him that the Lord had brought him to Myrtle Beach, and that even though it may not have been under the happiest of circumstances, he was there for a purpose.

"Yea, I guess I am," the boy responded, "I'm glad I was here today too."

THE PATH HE CHOOSES

Asheigh was right. She is a miracle—we all are!

Friend, you may not be walking the pathway you would have chosen for your life or feel you were placed on this earth for a divine reason.

But keep looking up because a miracle may just "drop" your way!

Eight

GOOD GRIEF

*Y*ou probably heard this when you were a kid: "This is going to hurt me more than it is you."

Yeah, right!

I had it said to me several times before spankings, but when it occurred I thought it definitely hurt me more—because I was the one wearing red stripes on my derriere!

Now that I am a mother, I understand the phrase. No, it didn't physically hurt me more to spank my children; it just broke my heart on the few occasions when I felt it was absolutely necessary for one of them. I grieved all night long.

The first time I spanked Alex, he had run out into the street in the path of an oncoming car—after he had specifically been warned not to leave the yard.

I didn't sleep the whole night, but it was my "trump

card," and I knew my son needed to understand that he could not disobey me, especially when his safety was at stake.

TURN IT AROUND

In truth we can cause our heavenly Father and His Holy Spirit to grieve, just as we do to our earthly parents.

When I looked up the term *grief,* it read "to bring sorrow."Ouch! I can bring sorrow to God every time I disobey Him.

_____ ❧ _____

Ouch! I can bring sorrow to God every time I disobey Him .

If that is the case then how can there be "good" grief?

Reflect back for a moment to the times we received a spanking ourselves. It was probably because we didn't listen to our parents. We disobeyed. And even though I felt I always argued my case eloquently and won, the fact remained I refused to follow orders.

Once I got over the initial anger of being spanked and realized it was to correct my behavior, I was always sorry for my actions. I would quickly ask for forgiveness.

This is the key. Grief can be good if we repent of our sins. It can allow us to see where we have fallen short.

THE FORGIVENESS FACTOR

Let me suggest you pause where you are and ask the Holy Spirit to forgive you of the times you have caused Him anguish. Remember, the Bible tells us, "And do not grieve the Holy Spirit of God with whom you were sealed for the day of redemption" (Ephesians 4:30).

Allow the Lord's forgiveness to fill you with peace. That's good grief!

Nine

THOSE BLUE FOOTPRINTS

*W*e all have fond memories, but some of our responses to events aren't always fondly remembered.

Our children were still very young when we moved into our present home. It was spring, a busy time of year for kids too.

We raced home from carpool one afternoon and Ashleigh had a friend over to play. Alex had a ton of homework and a baseball game that evening, and I needed to get them all fed. We'd only been in our home for two weeks so there were still plenty of boxes scattered all over the place.

Ashleigh ran down the stairs with her friend right behind her, holding a plastic tub full of art supplies. She called out, "Mommy, can we play art?"

I replied, "Sure, just go outside and try not to make a mess." I knew this would keep them out of my hair.

My daughter and her friend happily skipped outdoors. They were outside for over 30 minutes, and I didn't hear a peep out of them.

I finished cooking supper, my son completed his homework and got dressed for baseball, and I headed out to call the girls in to eat.

"WHAT HAVE YOU DONE?"

As I stepped out of the door, I couldn't believe my eyes. The girls had opened the blue paint from the art kit and proceeded to make blue footprints all over the driveway. Next, they made blue handprints, and finally ended up painting themselves completely blue. I saw two smurfs (remember those blue cartoon characters?) and squealed, "What have you done? You've made such a mess!"

The girls sweetly replied, "We painted."

I bellowed, "Get in the backyard right now and take your clothes off! I'm going to hose you down."

The girls sheepishly did as I asked. I quickly

followed and hosed them down while barking; "Don't get my new carpet dirty!"

I cleaned the girls off; we ate dinner, and got my son to his baseball game. The next day I drove the kids to school. Ashleigh wore blue shorts that matched the blue paint still in her ears!

When I returned to the house I noticed something as if for the first time. The sight took my breath away. All over the driveway I saw tiny little blue footprints that led to the backyard. It was then I realized that what had been a precious moment yesterday had turned into a barking session with me being the lead dog!

All over the driveway I saw tiny little blue footprints that led to the backyard.

WE DID IT AGAIN

Yes, we had new carpets, but I also had a water hose. A gentle laugh from Mommy would have surely embedded a sweeter memory in my daughter's heart.

That afternoon we painted our feet blue again. We *both* made lots of blue footprints. We laughed, hosed ourselves off, and enjoyed peanut butter sandwiches for supper.

Those small foot imprints have followed me in life. They have caused me to ask whether my actions were leading people to Christ-like principles or driving them away.

Ashleigh still talks fondly about her blue footprints, and the memory of them—plus the lesson I learned —still follows me.

Ten

SERMON ON THE MOUND

Have you ever asked. "When will it be my turn?" Our son, Alex, has certainly posed this question to me.

He is a good athlete; however, his quiet and reserved demeanor sometimes cause his athletic abilities to be overlooked.

Alex asked this question a few years ago, after he had sat on the bench and his team lost their third consecutive game. As his number one fan, I wanted to blame his coach, but I knew that wouldn't develop my son's character.

At home, I read this verse to him: "Trust in the Lord with all of your heart and lean not on your own understanding" (Proverbs 3:5). Then I explained that he would never be overlooked by God, so he needed to trust the Lord's wisdom, not his own.

I reminded Alex that he was part of a team and needed to cheer for them regardless of whether he played or not. Of course he grumbled, and I told him I knew this was difficult, but God expected us to keep a positive attitude, on or off the field. I kept telling him, "Keep working hard, support your teammates, and somehow things will work out for the best."

"No Way"

His next season game was scheduled against a much larger school than ours. However, after a couple of rough innings, our starting pitcher was pulled off the mound. But just before he was taken out, I heard the coach yell, "Alex in the bullpen."

"He's too young, and he doesn't have enough experience."

"No way," I thought. "He's too young, and he doesn't have enough experience."

But at the beginning of the third inning Alex ran out to the mound. All I could do was pray, and later he told me he prayed *too*!

80

The opposing team scored early, and then we tied the game. We kept it even until the top of the seventh inning when our team scored again. We were now ahead by one run.

Alex headed out to the mound for the bottom of the seventh inning. The first two batters struck out and the third batter hit the ball and made it safely to first base. The next batter was up. Alex pitched and he swung.

"Strike one," yelled the umpire. With the next pitch we heard "bam!" The ball soared towards third base and our third baseman caught it. We won!

Alex's teammates were crowding around, congratulating him, as were the parents. As we headed out to the car, the third baseman walked up to Alex and said, "It's all about you, *eight!*" (Alex's jersey number.)

My son replied, "I couldn't have won this game without you! You made me look good!"

"HE'S GOT IT!"

My heart skipped a beat, and I could almost hear God saying, "He's got it! This is about doing his best for his team, not being the best on the team!"

I was grateful Alex leaned on God for understanding, and the Lord did work things out for the best, and for our son.

That day he was the "Sermon on the Mound!"

Eleven

THE HORMONE ALIENS

*I*t seems that alien movies always get fantastic ratings at the box office. Being the mother of two teenagers, I'm not certain why anyone needs to pay to go to the movies to see creatures from outer space.

As I told a friend, "Moviegoers are welcome in my home—to witness live "hormone aliens."

Anyone with teenagers understands that one day you wake up, and your children have been taken over by irritable beings. Not only irritable, but also beings that are always right! When the takeover occurs, it can be a minute-by-minute change in behavior.

I feel justified in calling these body invaders the *hormone aliens*. However, when Alex turned sixteen, he started getting his body back! Well, I occasionally still see an attitude, intelligence second to none, and a roll of the eyes; however, he seems to be coming around.

But when Ashleigh turned thirteen it seemed she had been body-snatched! One day she was wearing ribbons and curls, then all of a sudden she wanted a particular ceramic straightening iron for her hair—and it cost $210. What's wrong with a ten-dollar curling iron?

AN OUTBURST IN THE HALLWAY

Not just parents catch the wrath of these aliens, but other teenagers can be subject to these extra-terrestrial mood swings. When my daughter made the cheerleading squad, she and her friends thought they were the cat's whiskers.

I was unaware that a cheerleader's hair is as important as the uniform. And bless my baseball-playing son's heart—he certainly didn't either.

Early one September morning I woke the children as usual. My first mistake! My daughter wanted to wake up extra early to shower and shampoo her hair, but neglected to tell anyone.

When she looked at the clock, and it was thirty minutes later than she expected, the transformation began. Ashleigh instantaneously morphed into the hormone alien. And my son was rolling out of bed into the hallway in her path just in time for the "force" to be with him. He ran into his sister as she was walking down the hall, and inadvertently knocked her hairbrush out of her hand.

_____ ❧ _____

Suddenly, I heard an outburst erupt from the hallway.

Suddenly, I heard an outburst erupt from the hallway. The next words were, "I'm sorry Ashleigh. I didn't mean to run into you—I was half asleep."

"Sorry?" she grumbled, "Is that all you can say?"

"GET OVER IT"

Evidently, she didn't think his apology was penitent enough and she began to chant in a galactic voice, "You messed me up, and now I'm going to have a bad hair day!"

Alex, still having some of those extra-terrestrial tendencies, rolled his eyes and replied, "Get over it! It's just hair!"

She barked back, "No, *you* get over it!"

He didn't say a word, but I could hear a giggle under his breath.

Alex had a good laugh, but he also learned the lesson that to the female species, it's not just mere hair, it is like paint to Picasso. It is the essence of our being!

Our family all survived the morning. And even now we still laugh at bad hair days.

Twelve

THE ACRONYM FANATIC

*W*hen it comes to acronyms, my husband is an absolute fanatic. He makes them up for everything.

Mike even creates acronyms for things that already have acronyms! For example, he loves the letters SAT. We all know it means Scholastic Aptitude Test, but he insists when taking our soccer-playing daughter to practice it means Soccer Aptitude Test.

We get a good laugh out of what he comes up with, but sometimes cringe at the ones that are corny.

My favorite acronym he uses is the one for Bible. He says B-I-B-L-E stands for **B**asic **I**nstructions **B**efore **L**eaving **E**arth. I love that. He didn't make it up, but he uses it all the time.

When you read all the "begats" in Scripture or try to interpret the book of Revelation, you may think there is nothing "basic" about the Bible. But stop for a moment and consider this. The word basic can mean "simple," but it can also be defined as "fundamental" —which means serving as an origin or source.

With this understanding, the Bible truly provides our Basic Instructions Before Leaving Earth.

THE SOURCE OF LIFE

God's Word tells us that before time began, Jesus, the *logos*, was the Word—the Alpha and Omega, the beginning and the end. He is our Source of life. Therefore, if we want to know how to conduct our lives, we should consult this Basic Instruction daily.

"All Scripture is God-breathed." In the words of the apostle Paul, "All Scripture is God-breathed and is useful for teaching, rebuking, correcting and training in righteousness" (2 Timothy 3:16).

This tells us that every single word in Scripture was inspired by our living and loving heavenly Father. As a result, the Bible can be used each and every day to teach us the path of life, for rebuke, to instruct us regarding how to change our disobedient ways, and to teach us the righteous (or right) way to live. Its pages cover it all!

WORTH OUR ENTHUSIASM

So before departing this planet, if we want to know how to experience redemption and live the abundant life, we must read and apply the Word of God. That is what's basic about the Bible.

I previously mentioned that my husband is a "fanatic" when it comes to letter associations. A fanatic is one who is "marked or moved by excessive enthusiasm and intense uncritical devotion."

It is a term we need to apply personally. So if I am going to be enthusiastic over anything, I pray it will always be about the Bible.

Thirteen

"Q" IS FOR CUTE?

*W*hen our kids were growing up they loved to play the "Jesus game." In case you haven't heard of this, it is where each player takes turns naming the attributes of the Lord by going through the alphabet.

One Saturday morning our son had an early out-of-town soccer game. We loaded up the car and headed down the road. As soon as we backed out of the driveway, Ashleigh, who was just four years old at the time, squealed, "Let's play the Jesus game!" The rest of us quickly agreed.

My son chimed in, "I'm first, mom you're second, dad you're third, and Ashleigh you're fourth."

"CAN I DO "Q"?

After setting the rules, which he loves to do, Alex

began with Jesus' attribute of being "A"—Amazing.

I added "B—Brilliance." And my husband offered "C—Comforter."

Ashleigh looked up and said, "I don't want to do "D." Can I do "Q"?

The three of us looked at each other, and agreed since it was our game, we could change the rules, and said, "Sure."

With a huge grin on her face, she proudly announced, "Q—God is Cute!"

A YOUNG GIRL'S REFLECTION

We giggled a little under our breath, and then it dawned on me. I had always dressed Ashleigh like a living baby doll. She wore gingham dresses, smocks, and outfits made of eyelet lace, and her beautiful loose curls were adorned with a bow to match each dress.

As long as Ashleigh could remember, when someone would see her they would comment, "Oh, she is so cute."

Ashleigh caught on very quickly they were saying this out of kindness and love for her—they were being nice.

As a little girl, she knew how much she adored Jesus, and loved Him with all her heart. So, with childlike faith, she associated Jesus with being cute. We didn't tell her any differently that day.

— ❧ —

I have this deep feeling in my heart that Jesus smiled when He heard Ashleigh.

I have this deep feeling in my heart that Jesus smiled when He heard Ashleigh, and her beautiful definition of Him. As she grew older, His love and adoration for her brought her to a saving faith.

SUCH IS THE KINGDOM

Jesus told His disciples, "Let the little children come to me, and do not hinder them, for the kingdom of God belongs to such as these. I tell you the truth, anyone who will not receive the kingdom of God like a little child will never enter it" (Mark 10:14-15).

Having pure faith like a child has nothing to do with hair bows or white eyelet dresses, it simply means that we come to Jesus with a childlike heart—and in Him we find salvation.

Ashleigh hopped out of the car that morning and

smiled, "Thank you for letting me change my letter. I just want to tell everybody that Jesus is cute"—or as she would spell it, "Qute."

Regardless, she wanted to let the world know about the One she adores and loves.

Fourteen

I'M DREAMING OF A WHITE CHRISTMAS —TREE

A long time ago I came to terms with the fact we wouldn't have a white Christmas. I live in Columbia, South Carolina.

Oh yeah, we did have a white Christmas once—I think it was in 1924—long before aerosol hairspray and the deterioration of the ozone layer. And since I'm a product of the 1980s, I spray my hair even though it does compromise the ozone layer! At least we look good, plus I've learned how to spray bad hair days away!

However, in Columbia there's little chance of a snow-scaped Christmas. Last year's holiday was cool, about 58 degrees, and we donned our parkas and went outside to watch the neighbors ride their new bicycles.

Actually, my husband and I were trying to get away from our son strumming his brand new electric guitar. Santa does not always think before he delivers!

Regardless of the climate in South Carolina, you can still enjoy a white Christmas—tree, that is.

MY CHRISTMAS PRAYER

As I detailed earlier, I grew up in an abusive home, and as a result spent most of my life trying to overcome the Christmas memories of my past. Most of them I choose not to remember.

When I was sixteen, I began dating a very nice young man, He literally had a *"Leave it to Beaver"* family and I loved every minute I was with them. His mother decorated every nook and cranny of their home, and when Christmas rolled around their house was decked out from top to bottom. It was the most beautiful home I'd ever seen. Every light was hung with love.

My favorite spot was their living room. I can still visualize the white Christmas tree adorned with pink decorations. For several years, I would stand at the foot of their festive tree and pray, "God give me a happy family and a white Christmas tree."

NOW IT'S MY TURN

Now the past is behind me and I am richly blessed. The Lord has brought me to a better place, I still love Christmas—but now it's my turn to brightly decorate our home.

I thank God every day that the dark corners of my childhood do not consume me. He has replaced the bitter with the sweet—with a wonderful husband and two beautiful children. (I've got a pictures if you'd like to see them!)

— ❦ —

I thank God every day that the dark corners of my childhood do not consume me.

Christmas is a time for celebrating new beginnings, the birth of our Savior. This is why I enjoy hanging every ornament and decoration on our white Christmas tree.

NEW EVERY MORNING

Today, you may be passing through a valley that has robbed you of joy and brought tears instead of triumph. I am asking you to look to the One who came to earth to lift us from the burdens of our past. "Because of the Lord's great love we are not consumed, for his compassions never fail. They are new every morning; great is your faithfulness" (Lamentations 3:22-23).

I don't know what mile marker you are passing along life's road. You may be longing for a happy home, a loving spouse, or to be reunited with a wayward child. God hears your prayers and you can trust in His mercies.

A Christmas tree—whatever the color—is a reminder that Christ still lives. And I pray He is living in your heart.

Fifteen

WHOSE GIFT?

*M*y husband anxiously opened his gift—just knowing it was the Polo shirt he'd picked out at the mall just two days before Christmas.

I was excited too! I knew I'd bought the right one and the right size. That's something to celebrate in itself! I usually spend a lot of time in January in the "return line."

He pulled the wrapping paper off, opened the box and bellowed out, "Whose gift is this?"

I looked in the box, and it was a size twelve (youth) gray Clemson sweatshirt. We both graduated from the University of South Carolina and Clemson is our rival school.

I looked at my husband and said, "Oh no!" In an instant I knew my friend's son was going to open a size large men's Polo shirt that same morning.

I quickly explained to Mike what we were already figuring out—I must have mixed up the gift tags. It was sort of funny, and sort of *not:* one of those awkward moments.

My husband was a little let down because he was looking forward to wearing his new shirt to his father's house that day, but even worse: a nine-year-old boy was going to be *very* disappointed. The Clemson sweatshirt was high on his "must have" list.

THE GREATEST PRESENT

What's the best gift you've ever received? Oh yes, birthday and Christmas presents are exciting, but my greatest present is the free gift I received from God when I accepted His Son, Jesus Christ, as my personal Lord and Savior.

What's the best gift you've ever received?

While what I received was free, it cost God separation from His Son—and cost His Son His very life. But they both believed we were worth it. "For God so loved the world that he sent his one and only Son, that whoever believes in him will not perish but have eternal life" (John 3:16).

YOUR GIFT IS WAITING

Have you accepted and opened your free gift from God? It will never be the wrong present, because the Lord doesn't mix up name tags. He knew you before you were ever born—and always remembers His children.

If you have never asked Jesus to come into your life and be your Lord and Savior, let me encourage you to pause where you are now and ask Him into your heart? And, if you have already received Christ, take a moment to thank God for His free gift—and share it with someone else today.

Our heavenly Father has more name tags available than the stars in the sky. So tell everyone you meet about the gift that is awaiting them.

Sixteen

MY NEW YEAR'S RESOLUTION

I'm going to lose weight. Wait a minute! Hasn't that been my New Year's resolution for five years now, and I've gained fifteen pounds—at least.

Something's not working! I start on January the second every year. I wait one day to get my collards and black-eyed peas in—just in case I run across a million dollars. And by January thirtieth I've cheated, more than once!

I just knew this year would be different. It has been. It's January second, and I've already cheated. I didn't even wait until the thirtieth.

Why is it I keep doing the same things over and over again? What I hate the most is what I do—and overeating is one of those "things."

Oh yes, I love how food tastes, but I despise the way it makes me feel when I have too much, and I really hate the way it makes me look, especially in jeans. So why is it I continue down this road?

"I CANNOT CARRY IT OUT"

One day I was reading the book of Romans and saw how Paul wrestled with similar problems. He wrote, "I do not understand what I do. For what I want to do I do not do, but what I hate I do...For I have the desire to do what is good, but I cannot carry it out. For what I do is not the good I want to do; no, the evil I do not want to do—this I keep on doing" (Romans 1:15, 18-10).

Scripture makes it clear that we all have sinned, and fall short of the glory of God (Romans 3:23). Why, because we have a sinful nature.

It's as if the chocolate starts calling me by name!

No matter how many times I try to forget that my children have Snicker's bars stored in the kitchen pantry, at midnight it's as if the chocolate starts calling me by name! I can't resist!

Sin operates almost identically. When we fail to surrender our sinful nature over to Jesus Christ we continually become entangled in iniquity—no matter how hard our flesh tries to break the cycle.

THE ANSWER

The same goes for what we "ought" to do. It's easy to do good to those who do good to us, but what about our enemy? What about showing favor to someone who has hurt you? What if the good you do for them allows them to advance over you or even become more successful? Do you still want to shower them with blessings?

I believe you see where I'm going. Without Jesus Christ we cannot overcome our sin, but "where sin increases, grace increases all the more" (Romans 5:20).

Tomorrow is a new day. I'll start my diet again. Right now I need to take a break. I think I hear my name being called from the kitchen pantry!

Seventeen

JUST A
STONE'S THROW!

*W*e like to say, "Innocent until proven guilty!"
Or sometimes it may be "Guilty even when you think
you're innocent."

At least that was our son's story when he was
fifteen.

Alex has been blessed with friends who are
identical twins, and they had just turned sixteen. Their
parents surprised them with a birthday party at a local
restaurant and the kids had a great time. Notice, I
called them "kids," even though they looked like men,
they were still boys (at heart) in men's skin.

After devouring their meal, some of the guys
decided to go outside for a little fresh air. My son
went with them. They are good boys, but don't

always make good decisions.

We chaperones watched as they went to the back parking area, which was really no more than a sand lot. It's an isolated area with only a brick fence that separates the restaurant from a row of houses.

THEY WERE SPEECHLESS!

After a few minutes one of the boys, picked up a stone and threw it at the garbage dumpster. It made a loud "ding" noise. Well that's all it took—soon they were all throwing stones.

Uncertain about the noise, a neighbor called the police, and on-duty officers were dispatched to the restaurant.

I looked up and the teens (with the fear of God written on their faces) were walking back into the restaurant with two police officers following. They were speechless!

Believing the officers were responding to a crime and not a noise violation, one of the boys blurted out, "Miss Cherie, the officers need to see you. We didn't do it! It wasn't us!"

The chaperones stepped outside to realize the

officers were there to find out what the "ding" noise was all about. They explained (trying to keep a straight face) that the boys needed to stay inside.

The police quickly realized that no real harm had been done, but the adults asked the officers to explain to the teenagers that they needed to respect property —even a garbage dumpster. Happy to oblige, the officers evidently scared the life out of them!

After their lecture, the boys finally admitted, "Yes, it *was* us!" Each young man apologized.

I think the boys learned a valuable lesson.

WE ARE ACCOUNTABLE

In many ways this incident mirrors life. We often start out with an innocent plan, but somewhere along the way detours occur and we make mistakes. Then, when we are "caught," our natural tendency is to quickly respond, "I didn't do it! It wasn't me!"

Our natural tendency is to quickly respond, "I didn't do it!"

Often our motives have no negative intentions, but it doesn't change the fact (as Alex can testify) that we may have offended or caused some problems along the way— and that makes us guilty.

We are accountable for *all* our actions, not just the well-meaning ones. This is why we are to admit our shortcomings to one another. As the Bible counsels, "Therefore confess your sins to each other and pray for each other so that you may be healed" (James 5:16).

If you do not have an accountability partner, pray that God will send you one because a "ding" in life may just be a stone's throw away!

Eighteen

"IF I ONLY HAD A BRAIN"

*C*hildren say the funniest things. Quite often inaccurate, but they sure make us smile!

A dear friend of mine attended a church in a small town in South Carolina. She wore many hats in the congregation—and one was that of being the youth minister.

While she was serving in this position, her senior pastor resigned and a young minster and his family were called to lead the church.

Because the new pastor was so busy on Sunday mornings, he never had the opportunity to pick his young son up from his Sunday school class.

One week the pastor decided he wanted to be like the other fathers and be waiting for his son. So he asked my friend and the music minister to begin the worship service and add a few more hymns to give him enough time to pick up his son, have him seated with his mother, and return to the pulpit.

"WHAT DID YOU LEARN?"

Everything went smoothly except that when the minister reached the platform he was laughing so hard he could hardly contain himself. It was contagious— and many of the church members began to giggle, not knowing why. But when he shared the circumstances of his laughter, the congregation burst into a full-blown roar.

Many of the church members began to giggle, not knowing why.

When the minister picked his little boy up from Sunday school, he asked the usual question, "What did you learn this morning?"

"DAD, YOU WON'T BELIEVE THIS."

With excitement in his voice, his son began to

share the creation story. He told his father he heard the greatest thing ever, and he wanted to share it with him because, in his own words, "Dad, you won't believe this."

The little boy proceeded to tell his father that God took dirt from the ground, blew on it, and out popped a man. Then he continued, "God made lots of animals, but no animal was a good helper for the man, so God put the man to bed and when he fell into a deep sleep, God opened him up, took out his brain, and made a woman!"

Go ahead. I laughed too!

A HAPPY HEART

Life gives us plenty to chuckle about so don't be timid over letting the lighter side of you show. Remember, King Solomon wrote, "A cheerful heart is good medicine, but a crushed spirit dries up the bones" (Proverbs 17:22).

Not only is laughter healing, believe it or not, it makes you beautiful! The Bible tells us, "A happy heart makes the face cheerful" (Proverbs 15:13).

In my book, the words cheerful and beautiful are one in the same.

If your heart is heavy today, remember the pastor's son. Or, you might think about all the men who complain, "If I only had a brain!"

Eighteen

LIFE COMES AT YOU FAST

*R*ecently my 6'3" teenage son got a stomach virus. He was really sick and needed to go to the doctor.

I attempted to help him into the office, but it was more like dragging him than helping. It seems like only yesterday, I carried him into the doctor's office perched on my hip, and now at best I was pulling him into the waiting area.

Immediately he was taken into an examining room, and as his long body dangled off both ends of the table, it hit me: my little boy was a young man.

It wouldn't be long until he would leave home and head for college. Suddenly, I forgot his stomach virus, and began to feel a wrenching knot in my own stomach. I wondered, "Have I prepared him? Have I taught him everything he needs to know? Is he ready to go out into the world?"

The look on my face must have changed because Alex looked over at me and asked, "Mom, are you okay?"

The tide has turned. He now checks on me. Instead of holding his hand in a parking lot when a stranger approaches, he places his arm around my shoulders, and tucks me under his side.

I whispered, "God, have I prepared him for life?"

He opens the car door for me to be seated, and then he goes around to the driver's seat.

How did this happen so quickly? My mind raced, as I whispered, "God, have I prepared him for life?"

I KNEW THE ANSWER

At that moment I heard God's tender voice reassuring me, *"Cherie, it is not humanly possible to prepare your children for all life has in store, however; I am fully able to be his sustainer. Now, have you done what I required of you as a parent?"*

I knew the answer. Even though I'd failed miserably at times, I knew that my children were aware of my weaknesses, and I had asked for their forgiveness on more than one occasion. But they also know where I draw my strength from, and yes, I do talk to my children about God when they are awake, when we walk down the road together, and as they lie down to sleep.

Even in the midst of my failures, God never skips a beat. He promises us that as our children step into the world, He will be by their side.

JUST MAKE THE CALL

Events have a way of zooming toward you at full speed. It can be bittersweet when your son becomes a man and your daughter becomes a woman. You're so proud of their accomplishments, but will forever miss carrying them on your hip or pushing them in a stroller.

Yes, life comes at you fast. If you are drowning you call for a lifeguard. If you are in a car accident you call your insurance agent. But no matter what happens—you can always call upon the Lord.

Thank God, He gives us His blessed assurance.

Twenty

WHAT'S IN YOUR WALLET?

*T*he very first time I met Mike, now my husband, was when a friend and I visited a large church in our city. He was teaching the Sunday school lesson in the class we attended.

It was a rather tough topic for singles: sexual purity.

What impressed me most was that he never seemed embarrassed, he laughed at appropriate times, and answered the sensitive questions even though he knew most people in the room were uncomfortable.

I left church that day thinking, "Wow, I'd love to date a guy like that!"

God hears our prayers. I dated Mike for fourteen months, and then we said our "I do's."

From the beginning, I was captivated by his calmness, confidence, and his ability to put others at ease, not to mention his good looks. But the attribute that Mike possesses which amazes me the most is how he is at peace. No matter what the situation, Mike never gets flustered; he remains calm.

BEHIND THE PICTURE

After we'd been married several years, and had two children, he insisted that I take Saturdays off, to have lunch with friends and enjoy a little "Mommy time."

One Saturday, I was rushing out the door, when I remembered I didn't have any cash, I grabbed Mike's wallet hoping to find a few dollars.

As I opened his wallet I saw my sophomore year college sorority photo in the first plastic picture slot. I smiled (not to mention I noticed a few changes in me!). It made me happy he still carries that photo.

Tucked behind the picture I spied a piece of worn paper. I pulled it out and in Mike's handwriting was Philippians 4:7, "And the peace of God, which transcends all understanding, will guard your hearts and minds in Christ Jesus."

There it was in a nutshell—the handwritten explanation for my husband's character, for his incredible peace—the Word of God.

Ever since then, whenever the energizer bunny works overtime in me, I remember what's in my husband's wallet—and it's not just a Visa Card!

Twenty-One

I DID IT MY WAY

*F*rank Sinatra and Elvis Presley made the song world famous, but every time I hear the lyrics it hits close to home. When it comes to how I touch the lives of people, I guess you could say, "I Did it My Way!"

It wasn't my intention to be a Christian comedienne, nor would it be the way I'd choose to share my faith, but friends and ministry partners kept telling me I needed to try comedy because they thought I was funny.

To be honest, I found this form of communication a little intimidating. What if the audience didn't laugh? However, it was through the greatest trial of my life, my battle with ovarian cancer, that I finally surrendered to God's will and embraced Christian comedy.

Genesis 21:6 says it best: "God has brought me

laughter, and everyone who hears about this will laugh with me."

Note, it doesn't say that Cherie Nettles is funny. It says God has brought me laughter, and because of this, I can help people smile.

YOU'RE EQUIPPED

I constantly remind others, if the Lord can use me, think of what He can accomplish through you.

What is God calling you to do today? Are you hesitant about answering His leading? Trust me when I say that He has already equipped you through Jesus Christ to answer His call.

If the Lord can use me, think of what He can accomplish through you. Will you flop sometimes? Absolutely! But I just use my flops for my next comedy routine. It works every time!

What has amazed me the most is the way the Lord uses His call for our lives to bring glory to His Name?

I started my comedy routine in the church, but slowly the Lord began to provide opportunities in an ever widening circle.

ONE STIPULATION

When a secular group calls and inquires about me doing a comedy routine for their organization, I tell them I have one stipulation; that they allow me to share for at least two to five minutes *why* I do comedy. The reply has always been the same, "As long as you make them laugh, you can tell them anything you want."

I have stood in front of law firms, insurance companies, state and federal agencies and shared my story of God's call on my life. That means I've brought my faith to places I never would have been able to reach had I not heeded God's call.

JUST SAY "YES"

If you are struggling with answering the Lord's leading, do yourself a favor. Stop fighting and surrender to Him. You don't have to be an expert or even the best (trust me!) you just have to say, "Yes!" And God will do the rest.

His eyes are searching to and fro across the land

for those whose hearts are willing to obey Him. "The Lord does not look at the things man looks at. Man looks at the outward appearance, but the Lord looks at the heart" (1 Samuel 16:7).

So, what is your call? Answer it with the skills and talents the Lord has given. Then you'll be doing it your way!

Twenty-Two

HE WIPES AWAY
WHAT BUGS US

*L*et me take you back to Vacation Bible School days:

Deep and wide, deep and wide!
There's a fountain flowing deep and wide.

Do you remember stretching your arms as wide as possible while singing that song? From time to time I still find myself humming the tune, and a recent incident caused me to think about the "fountain" that is still flowing.

While we were doing some major yard work last summer, we ran out of insect repellent. My husband wanted to try the new and improved repellent wipes he'd heard about, so off to the store I went.

Typical me, I rushed in for a single purchase, but got carried away going up and down the aisles. Well, forty-five minutes, $200, and a wobbly shopping cart later, I realized I forgot the wipes.

Now weighed down, I pushed the out-of-line cart to the garden center where mosquito repellent *should* be found. I asked the cashier for the improved wipes and she replied, "Look on aisle three, and if they are not there, try sporting goods."

I went to aisle three. Not there, so over to sporting goods. Nope, not there either!

Back to the cashier: "Try the grocery section."

How logical—mosquito wipes with the eggs!

I'D HAD ENOUGH!

With panic rising, I headed over to groceries and found myself digging through the rat poison. Would that be *new and improved* enough for my husband?

My search was futile, so I lurched toward the check out register where I heard a little girl ask her mommy if I were her grandmother.

I'd had enough! I continued toward the checkout

line and there was the same cashier. She obviously noticed my desperation, and dared to ask, "Did you find the wipes?"

"Nope," was all I could say.

"You probably can't find them because they are seasonal," she explained.

"So I can buy a Christmas tree here in June, but not insect repellent?"

"LIFE MUST'VE BEEN GOOD"

Just then I heard, "Cherie! Cherie Plott (my maiden name), is that you?"

I recognized this slightly over-weight, balding man and began to think, "God, just let heaven open and swallow me whole before this older

"Lord, do I look that old?"

man tells me he went to high school with me. Lord, do I look that old?"

"Remember me?" he exclaimed. "We graduated together."

We reminisced for a minute then his next comment pierced my heart. "I remembered you by your sweet smile. Life must've been good to you!"

Good? Well, I didn't tell him about being diagnosed with rheumatoid arthritis at 17, my mother's failing health, and my encounter with ovarian cancer.

At that moment the eyes of my heart reminded me how God has allowed me to drink from the "wellspring of life," with a beautiful family, wonderful friends, and a purpose for getting out of bed every morning.

I smiled and responded, "Yes, God has been very good to me."

Looking back, I realize there was no need to be frustrated over the mosquito wipes.

Yes, the fountain is flowing. It is deep and it is wide. So take off your shoes, roll up your pantlegs, and jump right in!

Twenty-Three

A WALK TO REMEMBER

A few years ago, our family—including all the cousins, aunts, and uncles—were staying at a beach house during our vacation on the Carolina coast.

It was a rainy day, so we thought we'd make the best of it. We made sub sandwiches, popped-popcorn, and baked cookies, and rented a few movies. It was a blast!

The first film we watched was *A Walk to Remember*. It is a sweet-teenage-summer love story. However, the teens are thrown into an adult circumstance when the young girl finds out her cancer has reoccurred. The storyline keeps the couple together long enough to marry, but by summer's end the young girl dies.

It was very sad, but I couldn't bring myself to cry because my sister and my fifteen-year-old niece were wailing—I don't mean just a whimper it was a full-blown wail.

I know it sounds crazy, but the rest of us got tickled listening to them, and we started laughing. My sister and niece stomped out of the room calling us *cold-hearted meanies!*

— ❦ —

The rest of us got tickled listening to them.

"OUCH," we said, and then giggled again.

THE REAL WALK

The movie was titled perfectly. The young girl, dying of cancer, had lived her life for Christ, and was dying—yet still living for Jesus.

That is certainly a walk to remember, but do you ever think about the REAL walk that changed history? It was the steps Jesus Christ took to His own crucifixion. He was forced to carry His cross to Calvary, on which He was nailed to die.

Even before bearing the weight of His cross, God's Son had been scourged, which means being whipped and abused just short of death. Scripture teaches us that Christ was beaten beyond recognition. So in agony, our living, loving Savior took this life-changing walk: "Carrying his own cross, he went out to the place of the Skull (which in Aramaic is called Golgotha)" (John 19:17).

Christ endured pain and agony, with flesh literally hanging from His body.

THE MEMORY IS FOR US

It was all for you and me. Jesus, being the Alpha and the Omega, looked ahead two thousand years, and saw us. He could have stopped this brutality at any time, because He is omnipotent. But because God so loved the world, Jesus took this walk to remember.

Who is to remember? We are! The memory is for us, His children, His beloved servants. Because while we were sinners, Christ took this path so that we would not perish.

I pray you have taken the most important steps of life—your steps to salvation?

JOURNEY TO JOY

I shocked a friend recently when I told her, "I'd like to be pregnant again!"

"You've got to be kidding," she replied

Actually, I was only half serious. When Mike and I learned our first child was going to be a son, it was one of the most exhilarating times of my life.

Even with all the morning sickness, I prayed to see his face, then to enjoy his first birthday. In those early years, at least I knew where he was all the time!

With both of our children, I decided I wouldn't wait for landmarks. Instead I would delight in every minute of their growth. Those "minutes" have included long hours of baseball games, soccer matches, and cheerleading practice.

But how could I ask for more. I have had the thrill of watching them develop into a godly young man and woman.

MINUTE BY MINUTE

I pray you have learned to live for every moment along the way, not waiting for some ultimate objective to be reached.

As believers, it is my observation that we often miss the true work of Christ in our lives. We anticipate the end of a trial or the outcome of a success instead of focusing on the minute-by-minute sustenance of the Lord.

Please don't waste your life only waiting for some ultimate goal to be attained. Revel in even the smallest victory. Accept the good with the bad; grow from the reverses that disappoint you; and give back from the blessings you receive.

FOUR LIFE PRINCIPLES

I have often been asked, "Cherie, what are the precepts you live by that have kept you on the right path?"

I could list many—including my prayer time, reading God's Word, and being with my family. But in addition to these, let me share four simple points I put into practice each day. I call them "The Living, Loving, and Laughing Principles"

Principle #1: Connect With People

In our techno-savvy world we have email, BlackBerrys (not just the edible ones), instant messaging, Twittering, and a whole lot more. But, unfortunately, the one ingredient that has been thrown by the wayside is face-to-face interaction.

Believe me I count on technology to make things happen. Instead of mailing a contract for a speaking engagement in Missouri or Montana and waiting for a "snail mail" reply, I email the agreement and have a scanned, signed copy back in a few minutes.

The one ingredient that has been thrown by the wayside is face-to-face interaction.

But given the choice, I'd much rather have personal communication.

I make it my goal to spend "physical" time with at least ten people every week. I am not referring to a casual "Hello," but ten individuals I actually engage in conversation with.

Enlarge your network. Set your person-to-person objective, then go for it. Connecting with individuals will give you the sense of "belonging." And after all, God created us for fellowship—with Him and with others.

Principle #2: Be Approachable

Open yourself up to others and allow yourself to be vulnerable. I'm not talking about being inappropriate —because you can easily lose friends and *not* influence others by being too candid (not to mention lose your job). But share from your personal life.

One of my signature comedy bits is when I talk about a time I was trying to keep warm while standing in line at a theme park.

It was a cold fall night in the mountains of North Carolina. We were at "Tweetsie Railroad" waiting to ride the last "Ghost Train" of the evening. It circles the mountain at midnight. Of course, that was the train my children wanted to be on.

I couldn't take the cold any longer. I reached my arm around my husbands waist and tenderly asked, "Sweetheart, give me your wallet, the concession stand is still open and I want some hot chocolate."

He was tight as a tick and didn't budge.

After a couple of minutes, I tenderly reached back with both arms around his waist—still looking around the corner for the train to arrive. Then I said in a firmer voice, "Sweetheart, give me your wallet, I'm cold."

"Sweetheart, give me your wallet, I'm cold."

I waited about thirty seconds; no response. I tightly kept both arms around his waist rested my head on his shoulder and whispered in his ear, "Give me your wallet!"

Unfortunately, I'd made a little mistake, because about that time I looked up, and from the far left corner where the restrooms were located, out walked my husband and two teenagers.

You've got it! My arms were wrapped around a complete stranger, and when my husband rounded the corner from the restrooms and saw me draped around another man, he barked, "Cherie Nettles what are you doing?"

Without missing a beat, I looked at my husband and replied, "Hush, five more minutes and I'll have this man's Visa card!"

137

"I BEG YOUR PARDON"

That mistaken identity moment was embarrassing. But when I share this story, I have many people come up and tell me their similar experience.

One of my favorites is the man who was trying to get his wife's attention at a dinner party. Bored, he wanted to leave early, but didn't want to appear obvious. So, he gently walked over to where she was standing—well, at least where she *had* been standing—and gave her a gentle pat on the bottom (yes, her derriere).

The woman with the same body frame, turned around and exclaimed, "I beg your pardon."

Now, dig yourself out of that one! Well, they couldn't leave now so they were forced to stay for dessert and coffee. It was a long night, but a guy's gotta do what a guy's gotta do—and that particular evening it was to endure the dinner party.

Principle #3: Laugh Often

Thankfully, we don't have to go searching for joy. As children of God, it is a fruit of the Spirit He has freely given to us (Galatians 5:22).

The Bible teaches that the Almighty has put "gladness" (which includes laughter and joy) in our hearts (Psalm 4:7).

Relax and learn to laugh at —— &°—— yourself! It's not only contagious, but *Relax and* scientifically is healing. Remember, "A *learn to laugh* cheerful heart is good medicine" *at yourself!* (Proverbs 17:22).

Research has proven that laughter contributes to lowering your blood pressure, increases endorphins in your body that promote overall good health and mentally gives you a sense of well-being. This is why laughter therapy is being used to treat depression and those with life-threatening illnesses.

If you want to be healthy and happy, look for humor in all circumstances. Since I actually found a few things to laugh over during my bout with cancer, I am asking you to look for the lighter side in your life too.

Principle #4: Keep Smiling

As a young girl I was told, "Smile and the world will

smile with you." I have no idea who said those words first, but they are certainly worth practicing.

I must admit there have been times when I had to literally paint a fake smile on my face, but it helped change the way I was feeling on the inside.

I mentioned earlier that I suffered from morning sickness when I was pregnant with our first child. It wasn't just a mild case of nausea. I was throwing up all day!

At the time I was teaching school and my students would ask, "Mrs. Nettles, How come you are so sick, so big, and yet you keep smiling at us?" (Middle schoolers will say anything.)

One day, I replied, "I smile so I won't throw up on you!"

I'm sure you've heard it said it takes fewer muscles to smile than to frown, and at my age I'm doing all I can to reduce the lines on my face!

As Mark Twain observed, "Wrinkles are merely lines where smiles have been."

May you be granted a wrinkle-a-day—they really will keep the doctor away!

"ON MY HONOR"

There's so much in life to give us headaches and

heartaches, so why take everything so seriously?

Remember, your body is the temple of God, and I'm sure He won't mind if you put on a couple of extra pounds. As we recited in the Girlfriend's Pledge:

We're just embellishing that temple in you and me,
For our world to see
That we know we're lookin' fine
So on my honor I promise to keep on growin'
my divine shrine!

Be assured I am joining you on this journey to joy.

For Additional Media Resources,
or to Schedule the Author for
Speaking Engagements, Contact:

Cherie Nettles
2125 Beaver Lane
West Columbia, SC 29169

Phone:
Email: cherienettles@sc.rr.com
Website: www.cherienettles.net